C000111682

Contents

Revival Phenomena

Colin Dye

Sovereign World

Sovereign World Ltd
PO Box 777
Tonbridge
Kent TN11 9XT
England

All Scripture references are taken from the New King James Version of the Bible, copyright © 1979 by Thomas Nelson Inc.

ISBN: 1 85240 187 7

Typeset by CRB Associates, Norwich
Printed in England by Clays Ltd, St Ives plc.

Foreword

Colin Dye's instrumentality under the hand of God, to touch *all* of London with truth and compassion, makes clear that he is a timely voice in today's Church. Here his research into the signs that have often accompanied God's mighty works, seizes our attention – and well might overthrow our temptation to arrogant preconceptions and humble our souls under His almighty hand, to cry: 'Pour out grace today, O Lord.'

Jack W. Hayford, DLitt
Senior Pastor
The Church On The Way
Van Nuys, California

'Do not quench the Spirit. Do not despise prophecies. Test all things; hold fast what is good.'

(1 Thessalonians 5:19–21)

Author's Note

Many people have noticed that – in the last few years – there has been an increase in spiritual phenomena. Some church leaders have even identified this as part of a new move of God's Spirit across the whole world.

The reports of these phenomena have prompted many questions to be asked. 'Are the phenomena really from God?' 'How do we assess whether they are biblical or not?' 'What do the phenomena mean?' 'How should we respond to them?'

In this book, I examine these important questions and try to point a way forward. I am writing as a church leader who has witnessed and experienced many of these phenomena both overseas and in the congregations I lead in London. My aim is simply to encourage a healthy acceptance of what is happening – whilst always maintaining all the necessary checks and balances.

An early form of this book was presented at the British Pentecostal Theological Conference in November 1995, under the title, 'Towards a biblical understanding of phenomena in revival.'

Colin Dye

'I, therefore, the prisoner of the Lord, beseech you to have a walk worthy of the calling with which you were called, with all lowliness and gentleness, with long-suffering, bearing with one another in love, endeavouring to keep the unity of the Spirit in the bond of peace.'   (Ephesians 4:1–3)

A Plea

This book is offered as one part of the continuing process towards a more accurate understanding of the biblical view on revival phenomena.

This is a very large topic, and my own experience is limited. If we are living when God's Spirit is moving in a fresh way, we can assume that what we have seen is only a small taste of what is to come. Certainly, I pray that my personal experience of revival – and the inevitable associated revival phenomena – will increase considerably in the coming years.

In this book, I have tried to show some awareness of many of the related issues. But I would be grateful if the book were not taken as a complete or final statement of my approach to the subject. I expect that God has many surprises in store for us all in the next twenty years!

Above all, I do not want what I have written to be used in any negative way against anyone who may differ from preliminary conclusions. We should always prize our unity most highly – especially at times of renewal and blessing. Our spiritual oneness is far too precious a gift to spoil.

'The antecedents, accompaniments, and results of revivals are always substantially the same as in the case of Pentecost.'   (Charles Finney, *Lectures on Revival*)

Preliminary Considerations

I am aware that this book will be read by people who come from a variety of national cultures and Christian traditions. Many of them will have quite different mental images of what is meant by the word *revival*.

What is revival?

In some parts of the world, *revival* is the word which is used to describe a gospel or evangelistic meeting. For example, some church leaders talk about organising a revival, while their British counterparts talk about arranging an evangelistic meeting. This is because they understand the word *revival* differently: both organise meetings at which they hope people will be converted, and both believe it is impossible to organise a visitation from God.

In some Christian traditions, *revival* is the word which is used to describe mass conversions in one geographic area during a limited period of time. So some groups talk about the Welsh Revival of 1904 or the Ulster Revival of 1859.

But other groups adhere to the strict meaning of the word and use it to describe a personal reviving of a believer by the Holy Spirit. They maintain that a non-believer cannot be 'revived'. So they use the word *awakening* to describe what many Christians call revival; and what they identify as revival, others classify as *renewal*.

Then there are those who associate revival with

excessive emotionalism, extreme hysteria and unaccept-able psychological manipulation.

The word 'revival' is not found in the Bible; although – as we will see – many types, examples and principles of revival are recorded in the Scriptures.

I believe that revival is more than large meetings, more than spiritual excitement, more than the dramatic renewal of believers, more than community impact, and more than mass conversions. These are some of the elements of revival, but – on their own – they do not merit the label 'revival'.

Powerful visitation

In this book, when I use the word revival, I mean 'a season of powerful visitation from God'. As far as I am concerned, revival is essentially a manifestation of God. It is a time when he reveals himself both in his absolute holiness and in his great power. It is God rolling up his sleeves – 'making bare his holy arm' – and working in extraordinary power on saints and sinners alike.

Although the term 'revival' properly belongs to the history of the church since the New Testament era, we can identify dominant elements which are present both in the New Testament church and in the revivals of history.

These centre on God acting through powerful manifest-ations of his presence – strengthening his church and awakening the world. Indeed, many features of revival mirror the New Testament experience of God: for example, conviction of sin, mass conversions, powerful spiritual encounters, revelations of God, assurance of salvation, spiritual fervour, community impact and a last-ing legacy for the church and society.

What phenomena can we expect in genuine revival?

All true revivals of church history have been marked by

unusual phenomena. Strange effects have been a feature of God's work in all the seasons of blessing – from early church revivals, through early monasticism, the Moravians and early Methodism, up to the Pentecostal revivals of this century.

Conversions

Records from every century show how the preachers in historic revivals regularly could not be heard above the cries of their congregations – and how many in their congregations lay flat on their faces during and after the meetings.

It seems that the conversion experience is often greatly intensified in revival. This experience includes all the usual biblical elements, but is characterised by a heightened experience of them.

Historical records frequently describe men and women experiencing intense periods of grief and mourning when they were overwhelmed by a conviction of sin and by their need for repentance and forgiveness. This was often followed by waves of extraordinary joy and excitement when the converts were overcome by a deep assurance of adoption and forgiveness.

For example, in his journal for 7th July 1739, John Wesley records:

> 'No sooner had Whitefield begun to invite all sinners to believe in Christ, than four persons sunk down close to him, almost in the same moment. One of them lay without either sense or motion. A second trembled exceedingly. The third had strong convulsions all over his body, but made no noise, unless by groans. The fourth, equally convulsed, called upon God, with strong cries and tears.'

There is an almost unlimited number of examples, from every century, of special periods of time when God's holiness and power were so intense that sinners turned to him in these dramatic ways.

Signs and wonders

There is often a strong element of signs in revivals. These are visible, usually supernatural, phenomena which point to the invisible, spiritual activity of God.

For example, the journal of David Brainerd for 8th August 1745 records:

> 'In the afternoon I preached to the Indians; their number was now about sixty-five persons.... Afterwards when I spoke to one and another more particularly, the power of God seemed to descend upon the assembly "like a rushing wind", and with an astonishing energy bore down all before it.
>
> I stood amazed at the influence that seized the audience almost universally, and could compare it to nothing more aptly than the irresistible force of a mighty torrent, or swelling deluge, that with its insupportable weight and pressure bears down and sweeps before it whatever is in its way. Almost all persons of all ages were bowed down with concern together and scarce one was able to withstand the shock of this surprising operation.'

Records of these sorts of signs are found in every century and every part of the world. They are similar to the phenomena which were experienced by the disciples on the day of Pentecost. Then, the sound of a mighty, rushing wind and the appearance of flames of fire were the outward and visible signs of the coming of the Holy Spirit. These signs pointed to the death, resurrection and ascension of Jesus.

Acts 2:12 reports that the crowds were *all amazed and perplexed, saying one to another, "Whatever could this mean?"* But when Peter responded to their question, he did not analyse or explain the phenomena; instead he pointed to their true significance.

Brainerd, in his journal, whilst admitting that 'I must say I never saw any day like it in all respects,' describes the phenomena in only five lines. He then fills eighty-two lines with a detailed description of the Indians' responses to God.

We must always beware of the danger of over-analysing a sign, rather than establishing its importance and meaning.

Gifts of the Spirit

Supernatural, spiritual gifts have featured prominently in most of the revivals throughout history. Prophecies, healings, tongues and miracles are recorded in every tradition and century – especially in this century's Pentecostal revivals.

For example, during the remarkable 1542 revival at Goa, in India, a Spanish monk wrote to his superior to report:

'I went into a village full of idolaters, and preached Jesus Christ to them, but the inhabitants would not change their religion without the leave of their lord. Their obstinacy yielded to the force of the miracles by which God was pleased to manifest his truth to them. A woman who had been three days in the pains of childbirth without being eased by any remedies was immediately delivered and recovered when she responded to the preaching of Jesus Christ.

Upon this miracle, not only that family, but most of the chief persons of the region heartily embraced the faith.'

In the Cevenne revival at the end of the seventeenth century, more than three hundred children spoke in tongues and prophesied with astonishing power and accuracy. This move of God's Spirit lasted for over ten years, before it was forcibly subdued by the French Army in 1711 and the children were either executed or transported.

During the eighteenth century, the gift of tongues featured in the Quaker revival in North America, the Jansenist revival in France, the Methodist revival in Britain and – especially – the Moravian revival in Germany and wherever their amazing world-wide missionary activity took them.

An anonymous critic of Count Zinzendorf, the leader of the Moravians, wrote that:

> 'He and his followers were great dealers in the Spirit and affected strange convulsive heavings and unnatural postures. And in one of these fits they commonly broke into some disconnected jargon, which they often passed upon the vulgar as the exuberant and resistless evacuations of the Spirit, and other such enthusiastic stuff.'

Many supporters of what is known as 'the Toronto Blessing' have looked to the eighteenth century American revivals of Jonathan Edwards (a close friend of David Brainerd) to support the phenomena associated with 'Toronto'.

I find this rather strange, as there are far more parallels to be drawn with the early days of Pentecostalism. Edwards, for example, seems to have rejected the miraculous, visions and prophecies. The present move of God is, in reality, an outgrowth of the Pentecostal revival at the turn of this century. Unfortunately, many conservative evangelicals continue to reject – or fail to recognise – the radical Pentecostalism which gave birth to most of the Third World revivals of this century, and paved the way for the more recent charismatic renewal in the mainline denominations.

Physical and emotional effects of the Spirit

Church history has well documented the many different ways that people have reacted to God's powerful and holy presence.

Everything that is happening today (and much, much more) has occurred before with remarkable similarity. The next two reports could come from any country and any century. They could even describe recent events in many churches.

'She could neither go nor stand, nor sit on her seat without being held up. After public service was over, she lay flat on the ground and would take no notice of, nor give any answer to, any that spoke to her. Thus she continued for many hours.'

'I don't know any other terms for describing or explaining it. Nor does the soul then know what to do, whether to speak or be silent, whether to laugh or to weep. This is a glorious foolishness, a heavenly madness where true wisdom is learnt; and it is for the soul a most delightful way of enjoying.'

(The first report is from New Jersey in the early eighteenth century: the second comes from sixteenth century Spain.)

There are leaders today who accept that unusual phenomena may accompany conversions, and that signs, wonders and spiritual gifts come from God. But they question the physical and emotional effects of the Spirit on people in revival.

In this book, therefore, I will now concentrate on these particular phenomena, offering a biblical analysis and framework for their consideration.

'Let us be very careful that we do not do violence to man's very nature and constitution: man reacts as a whole. And it is just folly to expect that he can react in the realm of the spiritual without anything happening to the rest of him, to the soul and to the body.'

(Dr Martyn Lloyd-Jones, *Revival*)

Physical and Emotional Effects
of the Spirit's Activity

Pentecostal and charismatic Christians are no strangers to the idea of physical effects resulting from the Holy Spirit's activity. They expect that the coming of the Spirit will normally be accompanied by some form of physical manifestation. For example, many of them believe that tongues, a form of prophetic speech, is a 'sign gift' which is given as evidence of baptism in the Spirit.

Spiritual gifts

Of course, no physical manifestation or spiritual gift – not even tongues – measures our spirituality. In 1 Corinthians 12:3, Paul offers the only acceptable measure of spirituality:

> 'No one speaking by the Spirit of God calls Jesus accursed, and no one can say that Jesus is Lord except by the Holy Spirit.'

In contrast to all the gifts which follow in Paul's teaching, a genuine acknowledgment of Jesus as Lord appears to be the crucial test of the Spirit's presence and activity.

Most Pentecostal and charismatic Christians are familiar with the range of spiritual gifts or manifestations that we can expect when the Holy Spirit is at work in the church.

The New Testament may not list every possible gift; and Jesus may send other ones which are not mentioned in Romans 12:3–8; Ephesians 4:7–16 and 1 Corinthians 12:1–11. But, in every case, it is clear what the spiritual gift is, and what the real purpose is of its manifestation.

Every spiritual gift is intended to build us together and up in Christ, to direct us as to his heart, mind and will; and to reveal Christ in some way – either to the church or to the world.

Physical effects

Throughout the Scriptures, there are clear indications of physical effects other than gifts taking place during powerful spiritual encounters.

For example, Exodus 34:29–35 records that Moses' encounter with God on Mount Sinai resulted in a facial glow which was visible to all who saw him. In 2 Corinthians 3:7–18, Paul suggests the possibility that the faces of those who receive the Spirit will reflect the brightness of the Lord in a greater way than Moses. It is not clear whether Paul means a literal glow; but Matthew 17:2 and Luke 9:29 describe just such a physical effect at the transfiguration, and Acts 6:15 mentions something similar at the trial of Stephen.

On the day of Pentecost, Peter told the Jerusalem crowd – in Acts 2:33 – that they had *'seen and heard'* the outpouring of the Spirit. As the people had not seen the cloven tongues of fire, there must have been some other visible, physical sign of the Spirit's activity – as well as the prophetic speech. Perhaps the crowds saw something which made them think the believers were drunk.

Many charismatics have noticed that the faces of some people do glow when they have been anointed with the Spirit. This is not a fluorescence, but a radiant smile, a glistening of the eyes, a spiritual sheen which is obvious to all. Time and again, people say, 'He looks different', without realising the biblical basis for their observation.

Sometimes the bodily effect is a miraculous healing which affects the appearance. For example, Luke 1:64–67 and Acts 9:17–18 record that Zechariah's speech and Paul's sight returned simultaneously with their reception of the Spirit.

In the Old Testament, Ezekiel 1:28 and Daniel 8:17 show the prophets falling on their faces when they had dramatic encounters with God; and Jeremiah 23:9; Daniel 10:8–10 and Habakkuk 3:16 imply that the prophets trembled when they heard God speak to them.

All these physical effects cannot be called spiritual gifts; but this does not mean that they are not of God or lack significance. In this book, I refer to them as *physical and emotional effects* of the Spirit. However, a close examination may reveal that some effects are human reactions to the presence and working of God, whilst others are manifestations of the Spirit's presence in or through the human personality.

Recent occurrences

It is patently clear that, recently, there has been a significant increase in the number of people who are reacting physically and emotionally to the presence of the Holy Spirit.

In Christian meetings in the last few years, more and more men and women have been laughing and weeping, shaking and falling, leaping and lying prostrate; and recently an oil-like substance has been appearing on people's hands during worship.

Twenty years ago, these phenomena were almost unheard of outside the Pentecostal churches. However, they are now often reported – by both the Christian and the wider press – as occurring in churches of many different denominations.

In Britain, many of these phenomena began to occur at certain charismatic conferences held during the mid-eighties. Many church leaders from traditional denominations who attended, saw these phenomena for the first time.

Then in 1994 news came from Toronto, Canada of an even greater outbreak of laughing, falling and other phenomena. Notable Pentecostal ministries such as that of Rodney Howard-Browne came to the fore, and the 'new move of God' took hold in the USA, Britain and many other nations.

While it would be wrong to describe the present move of God in Britain and the USA in the mid-nineteen nineties as 'revival', it would be equally foolish to ignore the fact that many of the different elements of revival are taking place. We might not all be experiencing mass conversions yet, but many are certainly seeing more conversions than for a very long time. And we are starting to hear reports of significant numbers of conversions in a few locations.

So, if these phenomena are occurring when we are not in revival, what can we expect to happen when God visits us for a season in greater power and holiness?

These phenomena are happening today. We cannot ignore them. They may break out in your services – they have in mine! We must know what to make of them. Are they biblical? Are they of God? We need answers to these burning questions so that we are not distracted by peripheral matters when God does visit us for a season in revival blessing.

We can all agree that if these physical and emotional effects are contrary to the Bible, they cannot be of God. And we do not want them if they are not of God. But if they are of God, then I do want them – or, rather, I want what God is doing in, through and alongside them. Surely no Christian leader can ever afford to miss what God is doing in their day.

For many people, these phenomena are the 'sticking point'. Some godly believers regard the laughter and weeping, the convulsing and collapsing as offensive. They reject them, and so reject all that is associated with them. They reject the current move of God's Spirit.

Having examined the arguments presented by opponents of the present move, I suspect that they question the move simply because they cannot accept the phenomena. They find them embarrassing, distasteful, unseemly, culturally inappropriate, and rather frightening. Of course, this is usually hidden under a thick undergrowth of theological objection.

Dangers of studying the phenomena

It seems to me that there are two main dangers which must be kept uppermost in our minds whenever we are studying or speaking about these phenomena.

Over-emphasis

The first – and main – danger is that we over-emphasise them. Indeed, merely by examining them in this book we are already over-emphasising them. We are giving them a higher profile than they deserve.

For many believers, the phenomena are so dramatic and so unusual that we can be sidetracked by them. It is as if we think that the phenomena are the essence of revival or the goal of what God is doing.

We rarely learn from the mistakes and lessons of history. This is exactly what happened with regard to the gifts of God's Spirit, both at the turn of the century – after the birth of the Pentecostal movement – and again in the nineteen seventies, when Charismatic renewal was gathering pace.

Critics of the gifts sometimes forced those experiencing them onto the defensive. As a result, too much time was spent justifying the gifts rather than developing and using them constructively.

Most of the books written by supporters of the gifts in the nineteen seventies concentrated on proving their validity rather than on demonstrating their purpose. Similarly, the critics could hardly stop talking and writing about the gifts in an attempt to discredit them.

Instead of getting on with God's work, leaders and congregations prized their opinions more highly than their unity. They were divided because they concentrated on the phenomena of the gifts rather than on the function of the gifts.

Furthermore, those who received the gifts within the traditional denominations appeared reluctant to benefit from the counsel of leaders in Pentecostal denominations – who had more than half-a-century's experience to pass on.

Equally, some leaders within Pentecostal churches viewed the sudden 'fashion' for the gifts in the traditional churches with a mixture of emotions – and did not give themselves as fully as, perhaps, was appropriate.

Like the gifts, the present phenomena can be endlessly defended and defined. But in doing that, we must guard against the tendency to become so pre-occupied with our examinations and justifications that we miss their overall significance.

False impressions

The second main danger follows on from the first. By focusing too much on the phenomena, it is possible to convey two mistaken ideas.

Firstly, there is always a temptation in every area of the Christian life to under-emphasise God's grace. Too many construe the phenomena as rewards for spirituality. They imply that – if we have not experienced 'their' phenomena – it must be because of some sin in our lives!

It was so with spiritual gifts. They are just tools to help us carry out Christ's great commission more effectively. They are not given to entertain or thrill the saints. And – especially – they *never* measure our spirituality. They are grace-gifts which are given to worthy and unworthy alike.

Similarly, the current phenomena should not be seen as rewards for repentance or righteousness. They are by-products of the presence and activity of God. His grace means that he works among the hot, the cold and the lukewarm – but he has an especially soft spot for sinners!

The second false impression is that the presence of the phenomena means we have revival. People glance at history and see that these phenomena occurred in revival, so they leap to the false conclusion that the phenomena signify revival.

My view is that we are not experiencing revival. Renewal, maybe; blessing, quite certainly; but revival, not yet.

However, I find the present move to be so beneficial, with so many hallmarks of the Holy Spirit, that it could well be the preparation for revival – the beginning of something greater.

'Instead of people maltreated, wretched and poor, Jesus sees the ripe harvest field of God. "The harvest is great." It is ripe enough to be gathered into the barns. The hour has come for these poor and wretched folk to be fetched home to the kingdom of God.

Jesus beholds the promise of God descending on the multitudes. Where the scribes and zealots saw only a field trampled down, burnt and ravaged, Jesus sees the fields waving with corn and ripe for the kingdom of God.'

(Dietrich Bonhoeffer, *The Cost of Discipleship*)

The Need for a Biblical Study

We could examine the phenomena of revival, especially physical and emotional reactions to the Spirit, from several different perspectives. Each of them would be both valid and useful in understanding and evaluating revival phenomena.

Historical

The history of revivals could be studied in connection with the phenomena which commonly accompanied them.

We could examine the background and origin of revivals – establishing the social and spiritual conditions which prevailed immediately prior to the revival.

We could look to see if special prayer preceded the revivals – remembering William Sangster's assertion that 'passionate, pleading, persistent prayer is always the prelude to revival,' and Matthew Henry's dictum 'when God intends great mercy for his people, the first thing he does is set them a praying.'

We could study the course of the revivals, paying special attention to the part played by the phenomena which accompanied them. We could establish whether similar phenomena were present in revivals within different Christian traditions and centuries – and in revivals which occurred at the same time, but on different continents.

We could attempt to determine what caused the revivals to cease and the extent of their lasting impact on both the church and society.

We would pay special attention to the contemporary explanations of the phenomena, and people's reactions to them. We would want to establish what was viewed as excessive, and how leaders responded to criticism.

For example, we could try to find out if the Countess of Huntingdon was correct when she wrote to George Whitefield in April 1739. She maintained that he brought a damper on his meetings when he removed the people who cried out and fell down. She wrote:

> 'You are making a mistake. Don't be wiser than God. Let them cry out; it will do a great deal more good than your preaching.'

Philosophical

It would be an equally helpful approach to examine the nature of religious and spiritual experience.

We could try to establish how the modern western way of thinking has been shaped by both rationalism and philosophical materialism – the belief that matter is all that exists, or all that is important.

We could investigate the influence of the Greek dualistic idea that the spiritual realm cannot readily interact with the material world.

We could examine the significance of deistic thought – the notion that God the Creator established the Universe and then left it to run itself.

And we would be particularly interested to evaluate the influence of New Age mysticism – that there are non-rational experiences where the mind is rejected.

All these philosophical influences – and more – are present in our culture and educational processes. So it is inevitable that they will affect both the way we view spiritual phenomena and the way we experience them.

Sadly, many of us either ignore or are ignorant of our cultural and philosophical pre-conditioning. We do not realise that this colours our theological presuppositions.

It would be instructive to see how people in different ages – with quite different cultural attitudes and philosophical outlooks – had responded and reacted to revival phenomena.

Psychological

We are often unaware how our own psychological make-up affects the way we react to phenomena – both in ourselves and whilst observing it in others.

It seems to me that reactions against revival phenomena often have more to do with psychological subjectivity than theological objectivity. My observation is that opponents of the current move are usually highly subjective in their perception of those who are experiencing the phenomena.

Religious phenomena are an extremely interesting field of study for psychologists. There is a variety of psychological 'explanations' for everything from conversion to speaking in tongues – including all the current phenomena of shaking, laughing, falling and even 'oil' on hands.

Psychological study can help us to understand why humans react as they do in certain circumstances, and why there is a similarity of phenomena in different religions and cultures.

Such explanations, however, do not undermine the validity of genuine spiritual experience. Please appreciate that to explain something is not necessarily to explain it away.

Behavioural sciences can help us to make sense of revival phenomena. For example, in *Signs of Revival*, Dr Patrick Dixon compares the present phenomena with the recognised psychological experiences of altered states of consciousness. He also analyses other psychological factors which operate through group dynamics and the physiological reactions that are associated with them.

Some people dismiss all the physical effects that are currently occurring as reactions which characterise individual personalities or temperaments. For example, it is often supposed that a reserved, controlled person will react accordingly, whereas an extrovert personality will be more open to an outward display.

However, a deeper psychological analysis would probably show that people of all races, temperaments and personality types respond in a similar way in the current move of God – as, it appears, has been the case in most outbreaks of revival.

Sociological

We could also examine revival phenomena, especially physical and emotional reactions to the Spirit, from the sociological perspective. Sociologists have always been fascinated by religious revivals, and they are very interested in what is happening in the contemporary religious scene.

As far as they are concerned, the current phenomena fit with observable sociological trends and patterns. Some sociologists consider all revival phenomena to be a 'manifestation of and release from the tensions that accompanied social change.'

In *Mega-Trends 2000*, John Naisbitt and Patricia Aburdene predict a resurgence of spirituality as a major stream of influence in the second half of the nineteen nineties.

They state that:

'unmistakeable signs of a world-wide and multi-denominational revival face us at the dawn of the twenty-first century.'

We should not be surprised by sociological analyses like this, but we must recognise that they do not reduce the move of God to humanly explainable sociological trends. This is because God works through these historical trends.

For example, it is doubtful whether the sixteenth-century Reformation would have come about had it not been for the European Renaissance which preceded it. Even if the Renaissance did not give rise to the Reformation itself, it was certainly the soil in which it flourished.

It is also foolish to study the great American revival of 1858–1860 without acknowledging the general social turmoil which preceded and surrounded it. With hindsight, it is possible to see that the slavery issue – which led to the Civil War of 1861–1865 – was a far greater factor in the revival than Christian leaders at the time would admit.

Likewise, the 1860 Indian revival occurred while the flames of the Indian Mutiny of 1857–1858 were still flickering.

It would be pointless to pretend that God has not often worked in special power at times of social confusion and breakdown. But it would be equally foolish to assert that he only worked at such times. For example, in the years 1859 and 1860 – as well as in North America and India – revival also broke out in places like Ireland, France, Sweden, England, Russia, Germany and Wales where there were no obviously unusual social conditions.

If God is at work in society at large, it should not be surprising to discover sociologists observing this. Indeed, church leaders should also be studying society very carefully in order to be ready for what God is doing.

If full-blown revival does come to Britain soon, it will not surprise me if social historians trace its roots back to February 1993, when two-year-old Jamie Bulger was brutally murdered by two children barely eight years older than himself. The incident shocked the nation. The Dunblane massacre of March 1996, when sixteen infants were shot dead in their school gymnasium, intensified this national shock.

Pundits and scholars were silenced – unable to explain what was happening. Politicians could offer no hope or guidance. The common-sense outcry was, 'What has happened to us that such things could take place in Britain today?'

Both tragedies drove home the realisation to ordinary men and women that they had been sold a lie. Although they could not articulate it as such, they intuitively grasped the truth that secular philosophy was bankrupt. The 'bubble' burst. People were ready for change. Evangelism is the most urgent need of our age to fill this social and intellectual vacuum.

Anthropological

The examination of religious beliefs and phenomena found in different people's groups would also produce helpful information for any study of revival. For religious phenomena which often appear bizarre in our modern western culture are a regular occurrence in other societies where the spiritual realm is more openly recognised.

This does not mean that we should adopt animistic world views and practices, or that the phenomena are essentially pagan. But anthropological studies can shed light on the rationalistic and materialistic impediments to the work of the Holy Spirit in our culture.

Theological

Theology is the knowledge and understanding of God, and of his relation to the world. But is our theology adequate to cope with what God has done and is doing in the world?

Throughout the centuries, Christian theology has developed in the light of God's activity in the world.

Events and circumstances have driven God's people back to the Bible as their source book for theology.

I am convinced that the Puritans were right when they said: 'God has fresh light ready to break forth from the word.'

If our theology has no place for revival, or for the phenomena accompanying it, then we need a new theology. If our orthodoxy squeezes out the dynamic activity of the Holy Spirit, it is hardly orthodoxy at all.

For all Christian people, the ultimate test of any revival phenomenon has to be Scripture. Even if a phenomenon passed the test of historical, sociological, philosophical and psychological analysis, it would have to be rejected if it failed the biblical test.

In this book, I am now going to concentrate exclusively on understanding and evaluating revival phenomena from a biblical perspective. Though the other areas of study are helpful, biblical study is – for me – the most crucial area of all.

'Back to the Bible or back to the jungle.'   (Luis Palau)

A Relevant Source Book on Revival

I am certain that a biblical study is the best way of approaching the different phenomena associated with revival.

But before we turn to the Scriptures, we need to be fully convinced that the Bible is relevant to all those revivals which have taken place since the New Testament era – and to those which are still to come.

The living word

Hebrews 4:12 states:

> 'the word of God is living and powerful, and sharper than any two-edged sword, piercing even to the division of soul and spirit, and of joints and marrow, and is a discerner of the thoughts and intents of the heart.'

The Bible, the written word of God, is living and active. It is a dynamic word which is relevant – not just for the historical situation that existed when it was written, but also for every period of history including our own modern world.

The Holy Spirit so inspired the many writers, compilers and editors of the Bible that we can consider him to be its ultimate author. He knew all our varied situations when he inspired the writers, and he speaks to us today through the Bible.

The sufficient word

I am convinced that the Bible is a full and sufficient written record of God's word to us.

2 Peter 1:3–4 states:

> *'his divine power has given to us all things that pertain to life and godliness, through the knowledge of him who called us by his own glory and virtue, by which have been given to us exceedingly great and precious promises, that through these you may be partakers of the divine nature.'*

This means that the Bible has great practical applicability: it is all-sufficient for all life and all godliness. Surely our theology should be equally practical. It must reflect the truth that the Bible is the ultimate tool in the task of knowing and glorifying God.

2 Timothy 3:15–17 makes this clear. In verse 15, Paul says that the Scriptures are *'able to make you wise for salvation.'* And salvation relates to everything which is associated with God's saving work in the world.

In verse 16, he states:

> *'all Scripture is given by inspiration of God and is profitable for doctrine, for reproof, for correction, for instruction in righteousness.'*

Scripture has been out-breathed by God. His word is useful. It has a practical, relevant, goal-orientated, four-fold use: teaching, rebuking, correcting and training.

In verse 17, Paul explains the biblical purpose as,

> *'that the man of God may be thoroughly equipped for every good work.'*

This means that the Bible is the all-sufficient source book for all aspects of the human relationship with God – for all time, including the present.

God encountered

Throughout the Scriptures, from Genesis to Revelation, the Holy Spirit has recorded many incidents when different people had powerful encounters with God. These encounters often had startling physical and emotional effects.

Even a cursory study of historical records shows that these biblical effects are remarkably similar to the phenomena which were experienced in the historical revivals, and are being experienced in the move of God today.

This is why the biblical study of the physical and emotional effects of the Spirit's activity is so important and so fruitful.

'I believe that the Word of God is of far greater authority than the Church; the which word only doth sufficiently show and teach us those things that in any wise concern our salvation, both what we ought to do and what to leave undone.

The same Word of God is the true pattern and perfect rule, after the which all faithful people ought to govern and order their lives, without turning either to the right hand or to the left hand, without changing anything thereof, without putting to it, or taking from it, knowing that all the works of God are perfect, but most chiefly his Word.'

(John Hooper, Bishop of Gloucester and Martyr)

Biblical Questions and Tests

A full biblical study of any move of God – whether in the past, present or future – would focus on several basic questions.

We would have to ask ourselves whether we can conclude, from a study of Scripture, that the phenomena taking place are of God. Or we might have to decide, from the biblical evidence, that God cannot be in them.

We would have to determine whether there are any biblical precedents or examples of the phenomena. We would need to establish if the physical and emotional effects were consistent with established biblical principles. And we would have to investigate whether there were clear biblical reasons why the phenomena could not be of God.

Is it biblical?

It seems to me that before we can reasonably conclude that a phenomenon is biblical we must first establish that it is at least consistent with the biblical revelation.

This is quite straightforward when there are clear biblical examples. But even if no biblical examples exist, it does not necessarily mean that a particular phenomenon is unbiblical. What matters is that the phenomena are consistent with established biblical principles which can be drawn from the biblical material.

I think it would be nonsense for us to expect that there should be a specific biblical example for everything we do in our life and relationship with God. I cannot agree with those leaders who suggest that this principle of interpretation is adequate for regulating human activities, but inappropriate for determining divine activities.

Surely this approach misunderstands the core nature of the Bible. God's written word is not a textbook in a limited sense. It is a living testimony, and a source book of reliable information which we can use for teaching, guiding and instructing believers – by both principle and precept.

Our God is sovereign, supernatural and infinitely creative. It seems logical to me, therefore, not to limit the range of his possible activities just to those which are specifically recorded or exemplified in the Scriptures.

Surely he can and will do as he pleases – though, of course, his actions will always be consistent with the way that his person and character are revealed in the Scriptures.

Principles and precepts

For example, the Bible does not record an example of every prayer that we will ever need to pray on every possible occasion. No biblical precept exists which instructs us to restrict our praying just to those prayers that we can find scattered throughout the Scriptures.

Instead, we can turn to the general principles about prayer and use them to guide our praying. Passages like Matthew 6:5–15 and Luke 11:1–13 provide principles which cover every need of prayer that we can possibly have.

Of course, we are encouraged when we find specific examples recorded in the Bible of people using prayers which fit our particular situation. But if no such scriptural example exists, we simply apply the principles of prayer to our situation as the Holy Spirit helps and directs.

I recognise that the Bible does not contain passages which provide specific principles about physical effects in the same way as it does about prayer and other matters. But it does contain general principles about the work of the Spirit and the manifestations of the Spirit which are relevant to the effects.

The point I am making is simply that God is not bound by the biblical examples of physical and emotional effects. We are encouraged when we find an example of a biblical person who reacted in the same way to the presence of God as someone today. But if no such precedent exists, we simply turn to the general biblical principles and apply them – with the Spirit's help and direction.

The word and the Spirit

The Bible is not merely a collection of texts which are drawn from several millennia, for the word of God stands in a dynamic relationship to the Spirit of God. I believe this means that we need more than an intellectual appreciation of the Scriptures according to the accepted grammatical, historical and theological principles of biblical interpretation.

I know that these principles are the essential beginnings of a biblical understanding, but I maintain that a mere human analysis of the Scriptures is inadequate. It seems to me that this is precisely what Jesus is saying in Matthew 22:29 when he criticises the Sadducees' approach to doctrine.

In replying to the Sadducees' trick question about the after-life, Jesus said:

> *'You are mistaken, not knowing the Scriptures nor the power of God.'*

Interestingly, the Greek text uses the passive form of the verb *'planao'* (to deceive). This suggests that Jesus meant the Sadducees had been led astray, or had been deceived, rather than that they simply had made a mistake. Jesus' words show that the Sadducees were not only intellectually mistaken about a scriptural detail, but that they had also been led astray by some power which existed outside of themselves.

The Sadducees' mistake was not just a word issue – knowing the Scriptures; it was also a power issue – knowing God's power. This suggests that Christian leaders who are not genuinely open to the Spirit – or who will not come alongside and thoroughly examine a move of God – must be careful before they condemn that move. Like the Sadducees, they may be supporting an inadequate understanding of the Bible – one which is based on a casual acquaintance with the word and is not rooted in the Spirit's power.

Throughout the ages there have always been those whose theological approach has been similar to that of the Sadducees. They – and their counterparts today – reject a theology which had been forged by a vital experience of the power of God.

The error of the Sadducees – and of many since then – is that they did not have an adequate understanding of the power and majesty of God. This kept them locked into the texts of Scripture, robbing the word of its vitality and its dynamic application to principles like the resurrection.

By contrast, in Matthew 22:31–32, Jesus pointed to two closely connected texts (Exodus 3:6 & 15) which – when properly understood with the help of the Spirit – show the truth of resurrection:

> *'But concerning the resurrection of the dead, have you not read what was spoken to you by God, saying, "I am the God of Abraham, the God of Isaac, and the God of Jacob?" God is not the God of the dead but the God of the living.'*

Paul also understood the need for the revelation of the Spirit in order to grasp spiritual truths and principles. His words in Ephesians 1:17–18 surely apply to our search for true scriptural principles about revival phenomena:

> '. . . *that the God of our Lord Jesus Christ, the Father of glory, may give to you the spirit of wisdom and revelation in the knowledge of him, the eyes of your understanding being enlightened; that you may know what is the hope of your calling, what are the riches of the glory of his inheritance in the saints.*'

Allowable or necessary?

Whenever we are considering whether a particular practice or experience is biblical or not, there is a subtle but far-reaching distinction which must be made.

If biblical examples of a particular experience exist, does it also mean that the experience is of necessity normative – that is, something we must all experience? If a practice or phenomenon is biblical under certain circumstances, does it also mean that – by definition – it is necessary under all circumstances?

And if something is biblically allowable, or even biblically commendable, does it also mean that it is biblically necessary?

This is clearly not so. There could be a whole range of biblically allowable experiences and reactions to the presence of God's Spirit, without those same experiences being commanded as necessary for all who experience God's Spirit.

For example, a passage like 2 Kings 13:20–21 is an uncomfortable incident for evangelicals – and is usually ignored at Pentecostal and charismatic healing conferences.

We dare not pretend that this incident is not a biblical example of an allowable supernatural phenomenon. But, obviously, we should not make the touching of dead prophets' bones a necessary practice for all who pray for the sick! Even so, perhaps we should rethink our attitude to the records of pre-Reformation revivals which describe people experiencing God's healing power in a similar way.

It is much the same with passages like Luke 8:44; Acts 5:15; 19:12 and James 5:14. People undoubtedly experienced God's power though tassels, shadows, aprons, handkerchiefs and oil – they are biblical examples of common pre- and post-Reformation revival phenomena. But it is almost as foolish to apply these words *indiscriminately* today without the prompting and power of the Spirit, as it is to touch a dead prophet's bones without the Spirit's direction.

There is mystery here. These biblical examples underline God's grace and sovereignty, and they should increase our openness to the genuine godly experiences of others. We should not dismiss such practices and phenomena out of hand without even investigating them, but we should not forcibly seek to emulate them.

The same two questions should be asked in any debate about current or future phenomena. Are the experiences biblically allowable? And, are they biblically necessary? The difference between the two is profound.

It is one thing to ask from a biblical perspective, '*May* I have the phenomenon?' It is quite a different matter to ask, '*Must* I have the phenomenon?'

Regardless of how powerfully the Spirit may be working in or through physical effects, it is surely wrong to say on scriptural grounds that one *must* experience these effects – unless the Bible clearly teaches that is the case.

Most Pentecostals believe the Scriptures teach that praying in tongues is the definitive sign gift which accompanies the baptism in the Spirit. However, it is not possible to argue that recipients of the baptism must experience all the other biblically allowable phenomena associated with it in order for their experience to be valid.

Is the fruit good?

Once it has been established that, in general, a practice or experience may be biblically allowable, it is still not clear whether any particular experience is actually of God. This is why the Bible puts forward another test.

In Matthew 7:20, Jesus said of the false prophets who were to come that, *'by their fruits you shall know them.'* This is a clear test based on the principle, *'a good tree cannot bear bad fruit, nor can a bad tree bear good fruit'* (Matthew 7:18). This means that we should not just look at spiritual gifts or manifestations when we are sifting the true from the false. These things are never the mark of genuine spirituality. Rather, we should test the spiritual fruit of the person who brings the prophecy or other spiritual gift. This should include both godly development and Christ-glorifying results in their ministry.

This 'fruit test' is also applicable to spiritual phenomena including physical and emotional effects. We could imagine all sorts of spiritual manifestations and physical effects which would be clearly contrary to scriptural principles; they are not the problem. We know that they are not of God. But we must also apply the principle of fruit to those experiences that do not contradict Scripture. What fruit is found in and through those who experience them? What results do they bring? This is not a question of mere pragmatism, that is, if it appears to bless people, then it's allowable. Rather, it is a matter of closely examining the longer term results of a spiritual experience to see if there has been some lasting fruit. If the Holy Spirit is at work in a willing heart, we will expect to see Christ honoured, holiness develop and a deeper love for God emerge. Above all, we will look for a greater power and effectiveness in Christian life and witness.

This is exactly the emphasis of Jesus in his teaching on false prophets in Matthew 7:21–23. He made it clear that certain miraculous signs and wonders – though biblical in themselves – were not to be taken as signs of a deep work of God in those who practised them. The most important thing was developing intimacy with God, and the obedience that flowed from that. The people concerned appeared to have great outward effects and gifts, but they were to be rejected by Christ because they failed the 'fruit test'. Please notice that the people were rejected, but their gifts were not questioned by Jesus. It is clear that God can 'draw a straight line with a crooked stick'. Presumably even Judas manifested the same spiritual power in healing and demonic expulsion along with the rest of the Apostles. This shows the absolute priority of developing and growing spiritual fruit. If a repeated spiritual experience does not produce good fruit, then the experience itself must be questioned or else the person experiencing must learn to allow the Spirit of God to touch the heart more deeply. On the other hand if a spiritual experience produces bad fruit then even if it is theoretically biblically allowable, it is to be rejected.

When we look back at the historic revivals, we rejoice at the well-documented good fruit of so many who fell, shook, laughed and cried. There were conversions, social impact, an increase in prayer and holy living, and so on. Equally, the records show that some who responded bodily to God's power bore no fruit – and that made their experience meaningless.

It is more difficult for observers to evaluate the fruit in a contemporary move of God, as – by definition – fruit takes some time to develop. However, there are many accounts of good fruit in the current move of God. These range from physical and emotional healings, to restored marriages and other improvements in lifestyle.

I have particularly noticed a deepening spirituality. People who have experienced some of the phenomena are speaking about a deeper love for Christ, a greater desire for the word and prayer, and an increasing readiness to witness for Christ.

When there is so much repentance and positive change –
so much developing good fruit – why is there still so much
criticism and rejection of what is happening?

My close analysis indicates that when someone is
persuaded that the phenomena are not of God, they
discount the evidence of good fruit and opt for an alterna-
tive explanation.

Some critics of the 'Toronto blessing' show their
prejudice and slack thinking by pointing out that several
New Age practices also give people peace; that some cults
restore marriages, and that many 'good results' come
from dubious sources. Convinced that the phenomena are
not of God, they reject the testimony of the fruit.

This is poor reasoning. Firstly, it ignores the distinc-
tively Christian fruit of conversions and a deepening
relationship with Christ. And, secondly, it presupposes
that the presence of a phenomenon or practice in a false
religion invalidates any occurrence in the true religion. It
makes more sense to believe that the counterfeit exists
only when the genuine is available.

However, the germ of truth in the argument is that the
basic question is biblical. If something can be proved to be
against Scripture, we must reject it no matter what the
benefits appear to be. The core question must be satisfac-
torily settled: are revival phenomena biblical?

The significance of the phenomena

There is another test of the phenomena, and that is to
determine their meaning or significance. I do not think
this can be easily dismissed, for I suspect that there could
be some real prophetic significance in the phenomena
which we are currently witnessing.

We have seen that the question asked on the day of
Pentecost was, 'What does this mean?' This is a question
we should be asking, alongside, 'Is this of God?'

We should be seeking God about the divine significance

of what we are seeing. What is he saying to us through these signs? Where do they fit into his plan for revival, restoration and the end-times?

In addition to this, it may be possible to trace some prophetic symbolism in the manifestations and phenomena.

For example, the prevalence of laughter could point to the release and joy found at a time of restoration – as in Isaiah 35:1 and Psalm 126:1–2. Genesis 21:2–6 shows that the name of Isaac, the child of the promise, means 'laughter'. Could this indicate that God is sending a new move which is in keeping with his promise to bless the nations?

Is it possible that the astonishing physical shaking of so many believers indicates God wants to shake his church into holy fear? Or might he be asking us to learn from the holy lifestyle of the early Quakers and Shakers – who shook in this way – and to prepare for the persecution that they endured?

Does the extraordinary weeping mean that God is urging us to mourn – personally for our own sin, corporately for our disunity, and representatively for the national sins of injustice, selfishness and greed? Is God calling us to move out into the world with his exceptional compassion for the outcasts, the poor and the broken-hearted in society?

The phenomena may merely point to God being at work, preparing us for revival. But, in practice, I am finding that God is using them to challenge our stubborn, proud and arrogant minds, and to expose the judgmental, critical condition of our hearts.

However, we must beware of reading too much into the phenomena – this is as much a temptation to some as rejecting them is to others. We simply must not select apparent parallels from the Bible at random. Instead, we must allow the voice of the Holy Spirit to speak through these actions – if he so chooses.

It would also be quite wrong to encourage the manifest-ation of the phenomena just because we believed them to be prophetic, for this could open the door to manipulation and to manufacturing the physical effects.

But all this must not be the heart of our evaluation of revival phenomena. We will not begin to consider their significance while we believe that God cannot be in them. Instead we will interpret them as mindless excess, as a dangerous diversion – or even as a demonic counterfeit. Once again, we see the need to go back to the Bible as our source.

Simplistic proof-texts

Finally, before we turn to the biblical material, we need one more word of caution. I strongly believe that the Bible should not be treated as though it were a collection of proof-texts.

Many critics of the 'Toronto' phenomena were quick to point out the 'proof-text' approach of some who accepted the manifestations. They felt that supporters were using isolated Scripture verses to justify particular phenomena.

However, this argument works both ways. Those who criticise people for using their collection of verses to proof-text phenomena cannot use the same principles of interpretation and the same verses to disprove the phenomena.

If the usual texts cannot be accepted as 'proof-texts' in favour of the phenomena, they must also be rejected as 'disproof-texts' against it.

Most of our scriptural information about God – his revelation and requirements – comes from dynamic encounters with him. A simplistic proof-text approach does not help us settle any matter of Christian doctrine or practice. And the same principle applies to questions about physical effects and revival phenomena.

For example, to suggest that Jeremiah 23:9 justifies today's 'shakers' is not a good biblical analysis or an acceptable interpretation. Nor can 'mooing' like a cow be justified by 1 Samuel 6:12, or by texts like 1 Samuel 15:14 which describe oxen carrying the ark of the covenant. Rather, we should try to get to the teaching which lies behind the texts and to the biblical principles that can be derived from them.

These examples may help us to understand something about what may happen to us if we have a powerful encounter with God like Jeremiah, and what God may say to us prophetically through animal imagery. But these verses do not sanction such practices in the church today.

Of course, the Bible will supply proof-texts of a kind for many areas of doctrine and practice – provided that these are studied in their immediate context and in the broad scope of all God's written revelation to us. However, there are many subjects which cannot be reduced to a pile of neatly organised proof-texts. Physical effects is just such a subject.

It is the task of hermeneutics and exegesis (establishing and applying principles of biblical interpretation) to tackle these issues with a great deal of care and thought. We will need the Holy Spirit's help and guidance – and great sensitivity to what he is saying through the Bible about a situation or subject.

It is usually helpful to look at how biblical principles apply to the subject and to work the matter out through Spirit-filled thinking. We need to go below the surface to look at the principles underlying the texts to see if they have any relevance to what is happening.

Commonly, the proof-text approach is a hasty wrong response to those who point to the lack of proof-texts in their attempt to discredit a move of God. We should avoid the simplistic approach of snatching at verses in order to prove that something is biblical. Understanding an issue biblically is far more than having a chapter and verse for each point.

Some of the Jews of Jesus' day rejected him not because there was no scriptural support for his mission and identity, but because the standard theology of their day did not have the right scriptures to hand.

If they had taken the time to search the Scriptures fully, they would have found much biblical support for who Jesus really was and what he had come to do. As we will now see, it is much the same with revival phenomena.

'The utterance of him who hears the words of God,
Who sees the vision of the Almighty,
Who falls down, with eyes opened wide.'

(Numbers 24:4)

Biblical Examples of Physical Effects

The Bible shows that the Holy Spirit's presence in or upon an individual or group of people can lead to certain physical and emotional phenomena taking place.

Some of these physical effects are recorded in a negative context like judgment. Others are in a positive context of spiritual communion or divine revelation. All of them are in the context of powerful encounters with God.

Each biblical example is not a proof-text which can be used to justify any past, present or future phenomena. For example, the current wave of shakings is unlikely to be the prophetic fulfilment of Ezekiel 38:20; and it might not be wise to use 1 Samuel 19:23–24 to justify similar behaviour today! These passages show that we must not ignore either the wider scriptural principles or the important 'fruit test'.

The biblical examples simply show that Scripture abounds with references to people who experienced physical manifestations, reactions or effects as they came into contact with the power of God.

When God visits in power and holiness, many strange or unusual things can happen to people. Some modern analysts – both critics and supporters of such phenomena – have dogmatically stated what the individuals recorded in Scripture were experiencing within themselves. But we do not know what they were thinking. We just have brief descriptions of their outward behaviour. However, it seems reasonable to conclude that most of their actions were the result of being overwhelmed by the awesome presence of God.

Falling

Falling is by far the most common physical reaction to God's presence – both in the Bible and in historic revivals. When God visits people, a common reaction is to fall to the ground in fear or awe. Sometimes this falling is voluntary, at other times it is involuntary.

- Genesis 17:3, 17. Abram fell on his face when the Lord appeared and spoke to him. God appeared to Abram many more times, but the Bible records him falling only here.
- Leviticus 9:24. All the people of Israel fell on their faces when the glory of the Lord appeared to them and holy fire consumed the offering.
- Numbers 16:22, 45; 20:6. Moses and Aaron fell on their faces when the Lord's glory appeared and God spoke to them.
- Numbers 22:31; 24:2, 4, 16. Balaam fell flat on his face when he saw the Angel of the Lord with a drawn sword in his hand, and when the Spirit came upon him.
- Deuteronomy 9:18, 25. Moses fell before the Lord as part of his fasting and intercession that God would not destroy Israel.
- Joshua 5:14. Joshua fell on his face to the earth and worshipped when God revealed his holiness.
- Joshua 7:6. Joshua and all the elders of Israel fell on their faces before God for several hours after the defeat at Ai.
- Judges 13:20. Manoah and his wife fell on their faces to the ground when the Angel of the Lord ascended in fire.
- 1 Samuel 19:24. Saul lay naked for a day and a night when the Spirit came upon him.

- Ezra 9:5. Ezra fell on his knees before God after fasting.
- Job 1:20. Job fell to the ground and worshipped on hearing that his children had died.
- Ezekiel 1:28; 3:23; 8:1–9:8; 43:1–5; 44:4. Ezekiel fell on his face when he saw the glory of the Lord.
- Daniel 8:17; 10:15. Daniel fell on his face when God spoke to him.
- Matthew 17:5–6. Peter, James and John fell on their faces when they heard God speak.
- Matthew 28:4. The guards at Christ's tomb became like dead men when they saw the angel.
- Mark 3:11; 9:20. Demon-possessed people fell down before Jesus whenever they saw him.
- Mark 5:22, 33; Luke 5:12. People in need of healing fell on their faces before Jesus.
- Mark 14:35. Jesus fell on the ground in prayer.
- John 18:6. The soldiers at Jesus' arrest fell when he spoke God's name.
- Acts 9:4; 22:7. Saul fell to the ground when he heard God speaking and saw God's glory.
- Revelation 1:17. John fell at Christ's feet as dead when he saw and heard him.
- Revelation 7:11; 11:16. The heavenly angels and elders fell on their faces and worshipped God.

In all of these situations, as God's word, presence or power was revealed, these people fell to the ground. Is it worth noting that they all seem to have fallen forwards, rather than backwards – as tends to happen today?

Some of the fallers spoke of physical weakness and of being overcome. Many of them were afraid. Some chose to fall; others fell involuntarily. A few seem to have fallen frequently. Ezekiel, for example, was obviously a great faller, while Abraham fell only once, and we have no record of Isaiah falling at all.

I recognise that many of these examples may have occurred in a different context from similar effects today.

But it is important that we note what happened to people as a result of God's powerful visitation.

Strength

1 Samuel 10:6 promises that,

> *'the Spirit of the Lord will come upon you, and you will prophesy with them and be turned into another man.'*

This was never more true than of Samson.

He was the last of Israel's Spirit-anointed Judges before Samuel, and Hebrews 11:32 lists him as one of the heroes of the faith. Samson was noted in Scripture for his God-given strength.

According to Judges 14:6, 19; 15:14; 16:28–30, his strength was a direct result of the presence of the Spirit of God. It was not his natural might, but a supernatural endowment of physical power from God.

These sorts of manifestations were unusual. It is interesting though, that David was anointed with the Spirit before his duel with Goliath.

It is important to realise that these manifestations of strength were specifically for the destruction of the enemy of the people of God. And God's announcement in Zechariah 4:6 – *'not by might nor by power, but by my Spirit says the Lord of Hosts'* – was spoken in the context of one of the Old Testament's four examples of a confrontation between the devil and a human being.

Maybe the significance of these manifestations is that they prophetically point to Christ's ministry in 1 John 3:8 – which he has passed on to us.

Boldness

There are many instances in Scripture where boldness came out of an encounter with God. In the Old Testament these usually involved boldness in battle or boldness in prophetic speech.

Micah 3:8 suggests that the Spirit was the source not only of the prophets' inspiration, but also of the courage to deliver the revelation.

> *'But truly I am full of power by the Spirit of the Lord, and of justice and might, to declare to Jacob his transgression and to Israel his sin. Now hear this . . . '*

Time and again we see those who had been anointed with the Spirit speaking boldly in situations of considerable personal danger, such as, for example, Moses addressing Pharaoh, David facing Goliath, Elijah confronting Ahab, and the prophet Micaiah in 1 Kings 22:13–28.

The Bible records Gideon being anointed with the Spirit in Judges 6:34. He had had a powerful encounter with God in 6:11–25, which gave him enough boldness to destroy Baal's altar and image at night. But, after the Spirit came upon him, he was filled with boldness to perform the mighty feats for which he is so well known.

Elisha's boldness, in 2 Kings 6:8–23, was linked to a spiritual vision of God's armies. Through prayer, he was able to pass this boldness onto his servant.

> *'His servant said to him, "Alas my master! What shall we do?" So he answered, "Do not fear, for those who are with us are more than those who are with them." And Elisha prayed, and said, "Lord, I pray, open his eyes that he may see." Then the Lord opened the eyes of the young man, and he saw. And behold, the mountain was full of horses and chariots of fire all around Elisha.'* (verses 15–17)

Boldness in the New Testament combined the two Old Testament characteristics. The Spirit anointed believers to speak God's words boldly in the context of the spiritual battle against the forces of the evil one.

John 7:25–26 reports Jesus speaking boldly in the context of people seeking to kill him. In Ephesians 6:19–20, Paul seeks prayer for boldness in the context of his great passage about spiritual warfare, and he comments on his boldness at a time of opposition in 1 Thessalonians 2:1–2. Immediately after teaching about the Spirit, 1 John 4:17 says that we have been given boldness 'in the day of judgment'.

We can see examples of this boldness throughout Acts, for example in 7:60; 9:27–29; 14:2–5; 19:8–9. Acts 4:23–31 summarises the biblical teaching on boldness and wraps it all together in the disciples' prayer for boldness.

> ' "Now, Lord, look on their threats, and grant to your servants that with all boldness they may speak your word, by stretching out your hand to heal, and that signs and wonders may be done through the name of your holy servant Jesus."*
>
> *And when they had prayed, the place where they were assembled together was shaken; and they were all filled with the Holy Spirit, and they spake the word of God with boldness.'*

Trembling and shaking

After fallings, tremblings and shakings are the second most common biblical reaction to a powerful encounter with God. This phenomenon has also been evident in most historic revivals since the late seventeenth century.

The Bible both describes the physical reactions of trembling and shaking and also prophesies that they will occur in the future. Sometimes God urges his people to shake and tremble. At other times – in both the Old and the New Testament – buildings shake when he moves on his people in power.

The Old Testament reports that people trembled when God spoke, when they read his word, when they worshipped, and when he manifested his presence in a visible way. It is important to note that the Old Testament shakings and tremblings are always associated with fear.

We can read examples of the tremblings in Exodus 15:15; Deuteronomy 2:25; 1 Samuel 14:15; 16:4; Ezra 9:4; 10:9; Job 4:14; 21:6; 37:1; Psalm 2:11; 55:5; 99:1; 119:120; Ecclesiastes 12:3; Isaiah 2:19–21; 6:4; 32:11; 64:2; 66:2–5; Jeremiah 5:22; 23:9; 33:9; Ezekiel 32:10; Daniel 5:19; 6:26; 10:10; Hosea 11:10–11; Joel 2:1; Habakkuk 3:16.

It is possible that some of the descriptions of tremblings may be figurative. But Jeremiah 23:9 reports such an intensity of physical movements that it is difficult to believe this can be anything other than a literal description.

> *'My heart within me is broken because of the prophets; all my bones shake. I am like a drunken man, and like a man whom wine has overcome, because of the Lord, and because of his holy words.'*

In the New Testament, Matthew 28:4 describes the guards shaking with fear at the resurrection, and Acts 4:31 reports that the building shook when the disciples were filled with God's Spirit.

Many of us have been used to hearing about Paul's 'fear and trembling'. But the wider biblical use of this phrase must make us wonder whether Paul literally trembled. The evidence of the Bible and recent historic revivals suggest that it is as reasonable to take 1 Corinthians 2:3 and 2 Corinthians 7:15 literally as it is to understand them as figurative.

> *'I was with you in weakness, in fear, and in much trembling.'*

> *'His affections are greater for you as he remembers the obedience of you all, how with fear and trembling you received him.'*

'Drunkenness'

It is obvious that caution is needed when using the word 'drunkenness' in connection with a spiritual experience. However, the presence of God seems to have come so strongly on the prophet in Jeremiah 23:9 that he was overwhelmed. The outward effects were similar to the bodily consequences of drunkenness.

In Acts 2:13, on the day of Pentecost, the disciples were accused by onlookers of being drunk. This was probably not because they were speaking with other tongues as they were the intelligible part of the phenomena. The tongues confused and amazed the onlookers only because they did not understand how uneducated disciples could speak so accurately in other languages and dialects.

We can only guess what it was about the disciples' behaviour which brought on the accusation of drunkenness. Perhaps they staggered around, fell to the ground, made a loud noise or laughed like people who are drunk.

One thing is certain: there was some physical manifestation or effect of the Spirit upon them which was obvious enough to attract attention and provoke a response. The simplest explanation of the onlookers' comment is that there was something about the disciples' actions which could lead to the claim that they were drunk.

Ephesians 5:18 is relevant to this phenomenon, although it is often wrongly quoted as a simplistic proof-text to justify 'spiritual drunkenness' today. When he wrote, *'don't be drunk with wine; rather be filled with the Spirit,'* Paul was making a negative comparison.

This verse comes at the end of a long section, beginning in Ephesians 4:17, in which Paul contrasts the old lifestyle with the new. Old behaviour patterns must be replaced by new ways of thinking and living. For example, truthfulness and honest work must replace lying and stealing.

When Paul mentions drunkenness, he shows that the Spirit-filled life is the opposite, positive lifestyle which releases us from any life-controlling problem. He is making a comparison and a contrast. In effect, he says, 'don't be controlled by alcohol, but come under the control of the Holy Spirit.'

The section which follows in Ephesians shows that Paul has a lifestyle in mind which begins with joyful praise, involves mutual submission and godly living, and includes spiritual warfare and prayer in the Spirit for all God's people.

The examples in Acts reveal that to be 'filled with the Spirit' means to come under the powerful influence of the Holy Spirit. Paul is urging us to be fully controlled and influenced by the Spirit as opposed to being controlled by alcohol. He is not referring to those people who have an occasional drink, but to those whose lives are dominated by their addiction.

In *Life in the Spirit*, Dr Martyn Lloyd-Jones suggests that Paul's linking of drunkenness to the Holy Spirit refers to the initial effect of the Spirit at Pentecost.

'I have no doubt that there was in the Apostle's mind at this point the memory of what he had been told about the reaction of the citizens of Jerusalem, on the day of Pentecost. Here were men suddenly filled with the Spirit; but certain people thought that they were drunk with new wine.'

If this is so, Paul was encouraging Christians to move on in their experience of the Spirit. He was asking them to move on from the manifestations which might accompany Spirit-filled experiences to a Spirit-filled lifestyle.

As Paul is dealing with the greater effects of the Spirit (a life under God's control), I do believe that it is valid to include drunken-like effects in the metaphor – but only as a lesser effect which may accompany a very special visitation.

Laughter

Laughter is one of the most therapeutic of all emotional reactions, and yet it can be repressed, particularly in modern 'religious' forms of Christianity.

The Bible describes three kinds of laughter. Firstly, there is the loud laughter of joyful surprise. Ecclesiastes 3:4 states there is a time to laugh like this, as well as a time to weep, but Ecclesiastes 7:3 reckons sorrow to be better than laughter.

In Job 8:21, Bildad promises Job that, if he behaves well, God will fill his mouth with laughter. Psalm 126:2 shows that the Jews laughed like this when they returned from exile: *'then our mouth was filled with laughter.'* And, in Luke 6:21, Jesus promises this gift to those who weep: *'Blessed are you who weep now, for you shall laugh.'*

Secondly, there is the laughter of wonder or incredulity. In Genesis 17:17 and 18:12, Abraham and Sarah laughed like this when God spoke to them and promised them a son. In Genesis 21:6 Sarah says, *'God has made me laugh.'*

The third form of laughter is the most common. This is the derisive or mocking laughter against an enemy which is found in Psalm 52:6. It may be surprising to modern ears, but Job 29:24, Psalm 2:4; 37:13 and 59:8 show that God himself laughs in this way.

God is the God of joy, and John 17:13 shows that God wants us to have the full measure of his joy. Laughter is one of the foremost expressions of that joy. Therefore, when people are touched by God, it should not surprise us that their mouths are filled with laughter and that they insist it was God who made them laugh.

Weeping

Crying, like laughter, is one of the most common ways of expressing human emotion. The Bible contains about one hundred and fifty examples of people weeping, including the famous occasion in John 11:35 when Jesus wept at Lazarus' death. These are the most relevant passages for our study:

Deuteronomy 1:45; Judges 2:4; 20:23–26; 21:2; 1 Samuel 1:10; 2 Samuel 12:22; 2 Kings 8:11–12; 20:3; 2 Chronicles 34:27; Ezra 3:12; 10:1; Nehemiah 1:4; 8:9; Psalm 69:10; 126:6; 137:1; Ecclesiastes 3:4; Isaiah 22:12; 30:19; 65:19; Jeremiah 9:1; Lamentations 1:16; Hosea 12:4; Luke 19:41; 22:62; John 11:35; Revelation 5:4.

In these scriptures, people weep before God with happiness and in mourning. They weep in confession, in repentance, in deep intercession, in sorrow, in trouble and in grief for the lost. They weep in worship, in God's presence, and for his work in people's lives.

They weep when they pray, when they hear God speak, when they read his word, when God appears before them, when he seems far away, when they are struggling with God in prayer, and when God prophetically shows them events which will soon take place.

These three passages give a flavour of the Bible material.

> *'So it was, when the Angel of the Lord spoke these words to all the children of Israel, that the people lifted up their voice and wept.'*　　　　　(Judges 2:4)

> *'The man of God wept, and Hazael said, "Why is my lord weeping?" And he answered, "Because I know the evil that you will do to the children of Israel."'*
> 　　　　　　　　　　　　　　　　(2 Kings 8:11–12)

> *'Now while Ezra was praying, and while he was confessing, weeping, and bowing down before the house of*

> *God, a very large congregation of men, women and*
> *children assembled to him from Israel; for the people*
> *wept very bitterly.'*   (Ezra 10:1)

There is no mention in the Bible of God the Father weeping, and – unlike laughter – there are clear promises that a time will come when there will be no more weeping. For example, in Isaiah 65:19, God states:

> *'I will rejoice in Jerusalem, and joy in my people; the*
> *voice of weeping shall no longer be heard in her, not the*
> *voice of crying.'*

Glowing

We have already noted that Moses' encounter with God on Mount Sinai resulted, in Exodus 34:29–35, in a facial glow which was visible to all who saw him.

Matthew 17:2 and Luke 9:29 show that this also happened at the transfiguration; Acts 6:15 describes something similar at the trial of Stephen; and 2 Corinthians 3:7–18 suggests that the faces of those who have received the Spirit will reflect the brightness of the Lord in a greater way than Moses.

Visions and trances

On several occasions in both the Old and New Testament, the Scriptures record people being caught up by the Spirit into a heavenly realm. In this experience, prophets were given insight into future events, and men were enabled by the Spirit to view the unseen spiritual world which surrounded them.

In whatever manner it occurred, their physical bodies were affected in some way by this supernatural encounter with God.

For example, in Genesis 15:1, the word of the Lord came to Abraham in a vision. In 2 Kings 6:17, Elisha's terrified servant was enabled to see that his master was surrounded by horses and chariots of fire. In Isaiah 6:1–13, Isaiah saw and heard the Lord sitting on his throne. In Ezekiel 1:1–2:3, the prophet had extraordinary visions of God. As well as these, Nathan, Daniel, Hosea, Obadiah, Nahum and Habakkuk describe their visions in detail in the Old Testament.

Furthermore, Joel 2:28 promises:

> *'it shall come to pass afterwards that I will pour out my Spirit on all flesh; your sons and daughters shall prophesy, your old men shall dream dreams, your young men shall see visions.'*

The New Testament reports Stephen's heavenly vision in Acts 7:55–56. Paul describes his vision in 2 Corinthians 12:1–4; and John sets down his in the book of Revelation.

Unusually, Peter's vision, in Acts 10:9–17, came while he was in a trance. It is also possible that Paul experienced a trance in 2 Corinthians 12. These two examples may be related to the Old Testament experiences of Adam and Abraham in Genesis 2:21 and 15:12.

Anger and strong words

In 1 Samuel 11:6 and John 2:13–22, Saul and Jesus were filled with the anger or zeal of the Lord – which came by the power of the Holy Spirit.

They saw a situation which grieved God or violated his holiness, and they responded out of a righteous indignation at its injustice. Their zeal was accompanied by a release of energy or by an empowerment to deal with the root of the provocation.

The biblical accounts of strong words directed by the Spirit are closely related to these passages. In Judges 5:23

an angel of the Lord instructed the prophetess and judge Deborah,

> *'"Curse Meroz," said the angel of the Lord, "Curse its inhabitants bitterly because they did not come to the help of the Lord, to the help of the Lord against the mighty."'*

The ten plagues on Egypt, in Exodus 7–11, were really ten curses which were prophetically announced by Moses and Aaron. These drastic effects – like those in Leviticus 10:1–2 and 2 Chronicles 26:16–21 – were experienced because the people concerned had profaned God in some way by their actions or attitudes.

In Joshua 6:26, Joshua cursed anyone who tried to rebuild Jericho: the outcome is seen, over 500 years later, in 1 Kings 16:34. Psalm 109 is a prophetic curse on Judas by David; and, in 2 Samuel 3:26–32, David cursed Joab and his descendants.

Perhaps Elisha's curse in 2 Kings 2:23–25 is the most dramatic Old Testament example of holy anger, strong words and swiftly executed judgment.

The New Testament records many similar examples. In Acts 5:7–11, Peter confronted the lying Sapphira:

> *'How is it that you have agreed together to test the Spirit of the Lord? Look, the feet of those who have buried your husband are at the door, and they will carry you out.'*

In response to these strong words, Sapphira dropped dead. Verse 11 must be one of the greatest understatements in the Bible!

Peter's words are an example of the Numbers 23:8 principle:

> *'How shall I curse whom God has not cursed?'*

In Acts 5:1–6, Peter did not curse Ananias, God struck him dead. But when Peter saw that God's curse was on the husband, he knew he had the authority to speak like that to the wife – if she met the same conditions.

The New Testament contains two examples of Paul making pronouncements against people. In Acts 13:4–12, he looked Elymas Magos in the face and pronounced temporary blindness on him because he was attempting to prevent the word of God from being spoken. And in Acts 23:1–5 he said to Ananias, *'God will strike you, you white-washed wall!'* History tells us that he was assassinated five years later while still in office as High Priest.

Most interestingly of all, in Mark 11:12–25, Jesus cursed a fruitless fig tree – a tree which, because it had leaves, had all the appearance of bearing fruit, but had none in reality. The disciples betrayed no surprise at Jesus' cursing. They were merely amazed at the short period of time which elapsed before the curse took effect. So Jesus taught them the secret of such Spirit-filled pronouncement.

Mobility and immobility

Perhaps the most remarkable physical effects of the Spirit are the biblical accounts of extraordinary travel.

Acts 8:39 states:

> *'the Spirit of the Lord caught Philip away, so that the eunuch saw him no more; and he went on his way rejoicing. But Philip was found at Azotus.'*

This sensational phenomenon is paralleled in the Old Testament by 1 Kings 18:12.

The three biblical takings into heaven of Enoch, Elijah and Jesus should also be considered as physical effects of the Spirit. Genesis 5:24; 2 Kings 2:1–11; and Acts 1:9 are all phenomena which can only be explained by the power of God.

The opposites of these examples are equally remarkable. 2 Chronicles 5:13–14 describes priests who were unable to minister in the temple, and 2 Chronicles 7:2 reports that some priests were unable to enter the temple.

> *'The priests could not continue ministering because of the cloud; for the glory of the Lord filled the house of God.'*

> *'And the priests could not enter the house of the Lord, because the glory of the Lord had filled the Lord's house.'*

These two examples, like nearly all the different biblical examples we have examined, have their counterparts in the historic revivals today.

Many people could have gone to these priests and said, 'It is written in the Levitical law to minister. How can this be of God, since he is interrupting his own word and worship?'

We cannot be sure exactly what form these physical reactions took, but they must have been visible and demonstrable for them to have been written down in this way. Perhaps some of the current reports of inability to speak and other similar effects fit into this category.

A variety of physical effects

When we try to make sense of all the different physical and emotional effects of the Spirit in the Scriptures, the first thing that must strike us is their enormous variety.

We have read about people experiencing very many different effects, yet it seems that there is no definitive list nor complete set of examples in the Bible. This means that a simplistic proof-text approach is not an adequate method of assessment.

Even the considerable number of fallings and trem-blings cannot be taken as examples to justify any current phenomena. The biblical examples simply help us to understand the kinds of things which may happen when God meets with us powerfully in visitation, conviction or prophetic revelation.

As has already been pointed out, many of the effects are human bodily reactions to the divine presence, rather than direct manifestations of the Spirit.

For example, some of the biblical fallings, shakings and weepings are clearly natural human reactions, whereas the utterances, glowings and visions are obvious manifesta-tions of the Spirit. However, it is impossible to tell whether some of the examples describe bodily effects or spiritual manifestations. The Bible does not distinguish between them – it is more concerned with the work of God and the resulting human fruit than with transient phenomena.

Therefore, if a bodily effect occurs today for which there is no biblical counterpart, it does not necessarily mean that it is not of God. Almost any effect would be biblically allowable – provided it was caused and accompanied by a genuine experience of God *and* there was the appropriate fruit.

A question of emphasis

The second fact which strikes us when we try to under-stand the biblical data is the small emphasis that the Scrip-tures place on the phenomena. They record even the most dramatic experiences in such a matter-of-fact way.

For example, Acts 8:26–40 uses twelve verses to describe the way Philip was guided by the Spirit to the eunuch, his conversation about the Scriptures, and the eunuch's conversion and baptism. But it then leaps over Philip's Spirit-empowered journey to Azotus in just two verses.

Jesus' transfiguration, in Luke 9:28–36, is probably the most dramatic power encounter in the Bible. Jesus' face was altered. His robe became white and glistening. Elijah and Moses appeared in glory and conversed with Jesus. God spoke audibly from the cloud of his presence.

Yet Luke slips this astonishing event between teaching about taking up the cross and the miraculous healing of a boy – giving these common incidents the same amount of coverage as the utterly unique transfiguration.

To modern eyes, Luke's summing up of the trans-figuration phenomena is almost incredible in its calculated under-statement:

> *'Peter, James and John saw his glory and the two men who stood with him.'*

He then reports that *'they told no one in those days any of the things they had seen.'*

Can you imagine any church keeping quiet today about such a manifestation? Unlike the Scriptures, we focus too much on the phenomena and not nearly enough on what God is doing.

Physical and emotional effects may be taken as evidence of a powerful encounter with God. But the biblical empha-sis is on the God who manifests himself, rather than on the immediate physical or emotional effect this has on the person involved.

Sometimes, physical effects are strongly implied in the scriptural account but hardly touched on, and – in some cases – not even explicitly mentioned. This shows the importance of meeting with God and seeking him for himself – rather than chasing a phenomenon for its own sake.

Strange but valid

A third interesting point about many of the biblical

examples is their sheer strangeness. If we are truly honest, some of them are not easily recognisable as being from God.

Many people today wrongly judge spiritual manifestations and physical effects on the supposition that they have to be instantly recognisable as evidence of God at work. But that is not the scriptural view.

We are to judge by testing the fruit of something, rather than by its immediate manifestation or by what we think God would or would not do in any given situation. This is particularly true for churches which have not experienced much in the way of bodily effects.

A study of the phenomena which accompany historic revivals shows that we should not be surprised if God does things which appear bizarre in comparison to 'normal' church life. On the other hand, we should not be surprised if a particular phenomenon occurs only once or a few times in some revivals, and not at all in others.

As far as we know, Philip did not habitually travel in his Acts 8:39 mode, Elisha cursed youths only once, Peter had but one trance, and Jeremiah shook like a drunk on just one occasion. Whereas, we also know that Ezekiel fell over several times, Samson manifested strength on many occasions and Paul pronounced judgement a couple of times.

The 'sign' we reported on page 14, in David Brainerd's ministry, occurred during 'a season of visitation' which lasted for just one month. As well as that 'sign', Brainerd also saw people falling, weeping, groaning and shaking. On 16th August 1745, he wrote:

> 'I never saw the work of God appear so independent of means as at this time. I discoursed to the people, and spoke, what I suppose, had a proper tendency to promote convictions. But God's manner of working upon them appeared so entirely supernatural and above means that I could scarce believe he used me as

an instrument, or what I spake as a means of carrying on his work. It seemed, as I thought, to have no connection with, nor dependence upon means in any respect. Although I could not but continue to use the means which I thought proper for the promotion of the work, yet God seemed, as I apprehended, to work entirely without them. I seemed to do nothing, and indeed to have nothing to do. God appeared to work entirely alone.'

The fallings, weepings, laughter, tremblings and holy wind did not appear either before this or after it in Brainerd's ministry. Likewise, the miraculous healing described on page 15 was also part of a season of blessing.

The monk had himself been healed through prayer in 1535, after surgeons had declared him incurable; but he saw no more evidence of miracles for the next seven years. However, in 1542 he saw God heal hundreds through prayer when he was part of the revival in India, and the blessing followed him when he ministered in Ceylon for several months.

However, the visitation ceased when he returned to India. He lived on for another ten years, preaching throughout the Far East. He saw thousands converted, but he experienced no more miracles.

Not normative

We have seen that to describe something as normative means that it is the expected norm for any Christian, anywhere and all the time. This is clearly not the case with the physical effects of the Holy Spirit's activity.

The biblical principles which can be drawn from the material we have examined show that such effects are biblical in the sense that they are biblically allowable.

But this does not mean that they *must* be present, only

that they *may* be present. And church history suggests that they are most likely to be present only during seasons of visitation which may last as little as one month, but may continue for several years. A correct balance will follow once this point has been grasped.

'Sundry old men were also in distress for their souls so that they could not refrain from weeping and crying aloud, and their bitter groans were the most convincing, as well as affecting evidence of the reality and depth of their inward anguish. God is powerfully at work among them!'   (Jonathan Edwards,
Vol. 3, The Works of President Edwards)

What Should We Make
of Physical Effects?

It seems to me that the way the Bible treats the physical and emotional effects of the Holy Spirit's activity – and the natural human responses to God's power – shows us how we should regard them.

Clearly, the actual encounter with Almighty God himself is the most important element in all this.

Seek God, not the effects

The biblical emphasis is never on the side-effects of an encounter with God – other than on long-term fruit.

For example, Acts 8 records the Samaritan believers' reception of the Holy Spirit. The different biblical descriptions of baptism in the Spirit indicate that this was usually a dynamic experience which was often accompanied by strong physical effects.

In some places we read of the Spirit 'coming upon' or 'falling upon' people. In other instances, whole buildings shook and there were clear visible manifestations. But, in Acts 8, there is no record of what the phenomena were in that particular instance. Pentecostals assume that tongues were manifested, but what else happened? It surely must have been an exceptionally powerful and impressive event – otherwise Simon the magician would not have wanted to purchase the ability to produce it to order.

Sadly, there appear to be some today who have fallen into the same trap as Simon. Dazzled by the phenomena, they are eager to know how they can reproduce them in their own situations – when they should be seeking only God.

The effects do not demonstrate spiritual depth

I am sure that we should not judge the depth of a spiritual experience by the nature of the physical effects it produces.

Some people are touched very deeply by God with little or no physical effect. While others have a very demonstrative physical experience which has little inner effect.

The leaders of the historic revivals were aware of this. For example, many strange and powerful effects of the Spirit came upon people during the eighteenth century revivals in Britain and North America. But leaders like John Wesley and Jonathan Edwards never viewed the effects as certain indicators of true spirituality.

In his journal, Wesley freely records the weepings, wailings and faintings and yet the danger of paying too much attention to these things is something he warns against,

'... as if these were essential to the inward work.'

Immediately after describing a powerful work of God involving weepings, groanings and fallings, Jonathan Edwards comments:

'True and genuine convictions of sin are daily promoted in many instances, and some are newly awakened from time to time, although some few, who felt a commotion in their passions in days past,

76

seem now to discover that their hearts were never duly affected.'

These leaders, in line with the teaching of Scripture, emphasised the need for genuine fruit as the real evidence of God at work.

The effects must not lead to elitism

We should also not compare our experiences with others as if we think that we have to experience the same effects as them. We are not inferior or less spiritual than them if we do not share their experiences. Nor are we more spiritual than others when we experience an abundance of physical effects.

These attitudes engender a spiritual elitism and foster false spirituality. I suspect that this is why the Bible records physical effects in such a matter-of-fact manner. The ultimate biblical Author knows that the effects measure nothing in men and women, they merely point to God's presence.

There is not a complete list of physical and emotional effects in the Bible, and the detail in each example is scant. The circumstances in every move of God are different, and the physical effects can vary from place to place, from person to person, and even from week to week.

Some features of a particular move may be present throughout the visitation. But some seem to come and go like the tides on a beach. Some phenomena have been present in revivals which occurred at the same time in locations that were thousands of miles apart. But some effects were unique to particular localities – and even to particular age groups.

New moves of God have introduced new phenomena. For example, from the New Testament days, significant tremblings seem not to be mentioned in any move of God until they are reported among the first Quakers at the end of the seventeenth century.

Equally, some phenomena seem to disappear with particular moves. For example, visions were by far the most commonly reported manifestation of the Spirit in the sixteenth century visitations, yet they have hardly been mentioned in the records of revivals since then.

The Bible is clear. God moves where and how he will. He is who he is, and he will be who he will be. We are to follow him, not the phenomena which may accompany his visitation.

John 3:8 states,

> *'The wind blows where it wishes, and you hear the sound of it, but cannot tell where it comes from and where it goes. So is everyone who is born of the Spirit.'*

Do not quench the Spirit

It hardly seems possible to me that Spirit-filled people who love the Lord would want to quench what God is doing. But it can and does happen.

God warns us in advance that – if we are not careful – we are likely to reject some of the things he does. His ways are not our ways. He does some very strange things and he uses some very strange 'vessels'. And he never seeks our approval of either his methods or his means.

To appreciate this point afresh – especially in the light of some of the contemporary reports of unusual phenomena – I recommend that, every now and then, we should re-read the stories of Samson and Elisha in Judges 13:1–16:31 and 2 Kings 2:1–8:15; 9:1–4; 13:14–21.

What would we make of the work of God's Spirit in and through these men if they were among us today? Would we accept their ministries or see fit to criticise them? How many of us would challenge or reject the phenomena which were associated with them? And how many of us would look beyond the phenomena and get close enough to them to evaluate the quality of their fruit?

Sadly, it is only too easy for us to be so affected by our cultural, philosophical and theological backgrounds that we cannot believe God can work in any way other than the one which fits our understanding. As a result, we quench the Spirit and scandalise the unity of Christ's body.

Test all things

There is a great need for wisdom whenever we are discerning spirits, applying scriptural tests and examining fruit. Just because there is some evidence that good fruit is developing, it does not mean that everything which occurs is of God.

Whenever the church is enjoying blessing – even a season of powerful visitation – there can be much fleshly activity and the possibility of demonic counterfeit. The devil will seek to use these to bring both confusion and disunity.

We must keep our eyes fixed on the Lord, avoid every wrong motive, deal with any false manifestation, and do as much as possible to remain at peace with those believers who are critical. Leaders cannot go along with everything; as Paul teaches, we have a responsibility to test everything.

1 Thessalonians 5:19–22 states:

> *'Do not quench the Spirit. Do not despise prophecies. Test all things; hold fast what is good. Abstain from every form of evil.'*

This means that we must learn to distinguish the genuine effects and manifestations from the fleshly and the counterfeit.

What is counterfeit?

In every move of God, there are always accusations of demonic counterfeit. This is a very serious matter. Such things do exist, but those believers who are genuinely seeking God and desiring to uphold the Lordship of Christ are protected by the Holy Spirit. Whenever the cross is proclaimed and the blood of Jesus Christ is honoured, counterfeit spirits cannot take hold.

Some believers worry that they might experience a counterfeit effect. But Luke 11:9–13 shows that our Father does not give us bad gifts. He *never* gives us stones when we ask him for bread. He *never* gives us evil things when we open our lives to him and ask him to bless us.

Of course, a Christian can become subject to demonic influence if they have never fully renounced and turned from a cultic or occult background – or if they fall into habitual sin and rebellion. But no Christian will manifest a counterfeit spirit if they are walking closely to the Lord. We have been anointed with the Spirit of truth!

Counterfeit manifestations claim to be the work of the Holy Spirit, but they are the work of a spirit which is demonic in origin. The devil uses them in his persistent attempts to deceive and destroy God's people.

Such manifestations occur because the devil is unable to create anything original – he can only imitate what God has made. In fact, the Scriptures teach that he has counterfeited many facets of God's work. There are false teachers, prophets, apostles, miracles, faith, doctrine, gospel, brethren and so on. A false, a counterfeit, an anti-Christ is behind all these.

The purpose of these counterfeits is simply to rob us of the genuine. Remember, the counterfeit is seen only when the real exists. Sadly, many believers have seen so few genuine manifestations of the Spirit that they cannot distinguish them from the counterfeit.

Some people worry that the presence of the demonic in

a meeting may mean that a counterfeit manifestation is at work. But the Holy Spirit will often expose the devil's work in a person's life in order to destroy it.

The demonic manifestations in Mark 1:21–28 and Acts 16:16–18 do not mean that the worship in the Capernaum synagogue or the Philippian prayer meeting was counterfeit. Exactly the opposite is true. The demonic manifestations proved that God's Spirit was at work in the meetings.

What is fleshly?

Fleshly manifestations are far more common than counterfeit ones – and probably do more harm to God's work. They are human-made substitutes for the genuine, and spring from our fleshly desires and motives, our pride, ambition and selfishness.

Some believers chase after emotional experiences. They are hungry for God, but they want him on *their* terms. They want a particular experience rather than whatever it is that God has for them. And so they force the experience onto themselves by manufacturing the phenomena or effects. Sadly, some – out of their need for attention or recognition – even appear to force an experience on others.

More often, what began as a genuine spiritual manifestation ends up as a fleshly show. Some of us are so concerned to show off, bless ourselves or be the centre of attention that we parade our experiences, boast about them, and exaggerate what God is doing.

There is always a danger of fleshly manifestations whenever we concentrate more on the phenomena than on God; whenever there is 'hype', exaggeration or overstatement; whenever we do not care if weaker brothers and sisters are being offended by our behaviour; and whenever there is any suggestion (no matter how subtle) that 'our move' is more special than any other.

What is genuine?

We have seen that 1 Corinthians 12:3 is the ultimate test of genuineness. All that the Spirit does is to glorify Jesus, to focus attention on him, to reveal his presence, purity and power. True submission to Jesus – in deed not word – is the distinguishing mark.

In 1 Corinthians 12–14, Paul teaches that all manifestations of the Spirit are given for the common good, to build up the body of Christ. They are not given for self, but for others. Genuine gifts of the Spirit have this 'other' focus – there is no sense of exhibitionism or drawing attention to the person.

Love is the foundation, the means and the goal of all Paul's teaching about the manifestation of spiritual gifts in these chapters. No matter how powerful a particular manifestation, if it is not manifested through and from love, it has no value. It is worthless.

I am sure that this 'love' principle should also be applied to physical and bodily effects. Everything that Paul teaches in 1 Corinthians 13 is relevant to all revival phenomena. His words in verses 4–7 apply equally to those experiencing the phenomena and to those observing the phenomena.

> *'Love does not parade itself, is not puffed up; does not behave rudely, does not seek its own, is not provoked, thinks no evil; does not rejoice in iniquity, but rejoices in truth; bears all things, believes all things, hopes all things, endures all things. Love never fails.'*

Without this sort of love, we are nothing. It makes no difference whether we are a supporter or a critic, whether we have experienced every possible phenomena, or none. If we have not love, we are nothing.

Those of us who want to experience only the genuine article will need to make sure that we are non-judgmental of others. We must take care that we do not reject the spiritual experiences of others too hastily. We must ensure that we are characterised by the Spirit's essential humility – and do not boast of a particular experience or parade it before others. We should always want other people to be blessed – with the blessing of God's choice, not ours. And we should do everything possible to preserve the unity of the Spirit.

Paul's teaching in 1 Corinthians 8 is crucial. At all times, we must

> *'beware lest somehow this liberty of yours should become a stumbling block to those who are weak.'*
>
> (verse 9)

In short, if we want the genuine we must make room for God – remembering that we must accept his move and not try to make it acceptable for ourselves. We must make room for others – remembering that 'knowledge puffs up, but love edifies'. And we must grow in grace – remembering that there is nothing we can do to make anything genuine happen: it is all grace or it is all nothing.

'I have myself frequently seen the preaching of the Word attended with so much power, and eternal things brought so near, that the feelings of the people could not be restrained. I have observed at such times an awful and breathless stillness pervading the assembly. I have heard a half-suppressed sigh rising from many a heart, and have seen many bathed in tears.

At other times I have heard loud sobbing in many parts of the church, while a deep solemnity pervaded the whole audience. I have also heard individuals cry aloud as if they had been pierced through with a dart. I have seen persons so overcome that they could not walk or stand; I have known believers who have been similarly affected through the fullness of their joy. I could name many of the humblest, meekest believers who cried out in the church under deep agony.

I am far from believing that these signs always issue in conversion, or that the Spirit of God does not often work in a more quiet manner. Sometimes, I believe, he comes like the pouring rain; sometimes like the gentle dew. Still I would humbly state my conviction that it is the duty of all who seek the salvation of souls to long and pray for such solemn times, when the arrows shall be sharp to the heart of the King's enemies, and our slumbering congregations shall be made to cry out, "Men and brethren, what shall we do?"'   (Robert Murray McCheyne)

Conclusions and Considerations

Too often, people are asked, 'are you for it or against it?' and are pushed into a conclusion concerning phenomena without the time for adequate reflection. In consequence, people become divided into opposing camps and the enemy rejoices at our disunity.

Through this book, I am asking people to reflect again on the nature of Spirit-inspired phenomena and to look afresh at the fruit in those touched by the most recent move of God.

As we have seen, the unfortunate use of proof-texts often aggravates the divisions, as do fleshly manifestations. People often seize on these unfortunate examples and use them to 'prove' that a move cannot be of God – whereas they have nothing to do with God, but are simply the foolish fleshly reactions of certain individuals.

People often make the false assumption that what God does is instantly recognisable as being of God. It is this assumption which – together with culturally pre-conditioned standards of what is acceptable – influences many people's initial responses to unusual phenomena.

But Jesus did not arrive in the expected way, did not act in the anticipated manner, and left in a highly unusual fashion. The Jews loved the Scriptures. They longed for the Messiah to come. And then they rejected him because he did not match their expectations. We need to be careful that we are not so 'correct' in our thinking that we miss his visitation in our day.

The evidence of the Bible and history clearly shows that God often intervenes supernaturally in the affairs of men and women. When people experience a powerful encounter with God, many things may happen. Therefore it is best not to exclude any possible physical effect or phenomenon merely because it is unusual or unacceptable to us personally.

I believe that now is the time for us to check our theology – before God sends revival. If our theology cannot accept what God is doing then we need to change, develop and expand our understanding. We need a theology which accepts that God can do what he wants, how he wants, where, when and through whom he wants – without our permission!

We have seen that revival phenomena are not normative, but this does not mean that we cannot expect them – especially when such phenomena are occurring. If God is working in a certain way, it is surely not wrong to expect him to work in us in that way, as long as we keep the matter in perspective.

As I have shown, it is too large a jump to say, 'I can prove to you from the Bible that this phenomenon can happen, therefore it must happen today.' But it is an even bigger jump to say, 'I can show you that it did happen in the Bible, but it must not happen today.'

We have glanced at the nature of revival and the associated phenomena. Some argue that the current 'blessing' cannot be revival from God because there are no mass conversions.

However, there are many conversions, and already there are a few reports of numbers which would not be out-of-place in an earlier revival.

But even if the blessing is not full-blooded revival, it may be the prelude to such a season of powerful visitation. Certainly, something is happening. There has been a change of spiritual climate. God is on the move, and our reaction to these 'pre-revival' phenomena is crucial.

In *Quenching the Spirit*, William DeArteaga points out that the greatest threat to revivals has never come from atheists or humanists, but from within the church.

He notes that the 1859 North American revival was seen by most New England clergy as merely a widespread epidemic of enthusiasm. What was needed was a return to sound theology. As opposition grew, so the revivals and conversions petered out. DeArteaga states:

> 'It seems much of what was defined as extremism, even by some of the Awakening defenders, was really an invitation by the Holy Spirit to further renewal and spiritual power. Christians as a whole, and certainly clergy, were not ready to receive that invitation.'

God forbid that the same thing should happen among us today. I pray that those who say, 'Look, there is no revival here,' are not actually inhibiting full revival. God's challenge to the first Christians in Acts was to move with, to keep in step with, the Spirit. God constantly challenged their pre-suppositions. I believe that he is doing the same to us today.

Practical suggestions

I want to close this book by making six practical suggestions for those who are experiencing physical and emotional effects of the Spirit – and also for those who will experience revival phenomena in the days to come

Seek God first

Some manifestations may be so unusual or different that we can be tempted to look at them or spend too much time analysing them.

It is vital that we avoid the danger of focusing on the effects of the Spirit. We must keep our eyes fixed on Jesus. It is also important that we don't chase after a particular experience as though it – in itself – has any value or importance. Equally, we must watch out that we do not attempt to 'market' an effect or hold it up as special.

Throughout the centuries, churches have turned God's work into a tradition. We must ensure that, when God has blessed us once in a particular way, we do not necessarily expect him to do so again – thus making a pattern or tradition out of it.

Please be aware that we can put God 'in a box'. If we do this, we can miss what the Spirit is doing when his wind blows in a different direction.

Always remember: we are called, first of all, to seek God and him alone. If any physical effects happen when he meets with us, they are up to him and unimportant. It is God – his word and his work – which matters.

Don't judge the spiritual depth of an encounter with God by the degree of the outward manifestation

People respond to God in different ways. Each person is unique, and God works in the lives of people in distinct ways at varied times.

Whilst receiving from God, someone feeling nothing can actually be being greatly touched by God. Others who experience strong outward manifestations may not actually retain anything of a deep or lasting nature. This may seem strange, but it is the openness of our hearts and spirits to the Spirit which makes a difference.

God sends the sun and the rain on the just and the unjust alike. It is possible to feel the warmth of God without making a response to him. The real work is done on the 'inside'. This is a mystery, and the fruit is seen only at a later date.

Please remember that some outward manifestations are

fleshly, as people seek to draw attention to themselves and their ministry rather than to the work of God.

For leaders, there may be a temptation to want to see physical effects – such as people falling over – either out of fleshly ambition or for fear of thinking that nothing is happening. This fear can be shared by members of the congregation who think that they are not receiving from God unless they fall down or show a manifestation.

In such ways, the work of God is discredited and hampered. But good teaching should eliminate these errors of thinking.

Do not manufacture physical effects, but do not resist what the Spirit may be doing

It is important that we relax, are open to the Holy Spirit, and are expectant. Some people are so careful not to be 'in the flesh' that they close themselves to the Spirit. Whereas others so want to receive that they actually imitate the actions and effects they have observed.

We must encourage people to be open to God, but we must not suggest how they should respond or give them a false impression of what may happen. Equally, we must take care not to go too far the other way.

A few have criticised those who prepare a space at the front of meetings for people to receive from God, saying that this is suggestive. It may be good common sense. If God has often worked in this way in the past, we can expect a particular effect to happen again – although we must not be disappointed or surprised if God does not choose to work in that way.

Quite often, the exposure and cure of our pride is higher on God's agenda than a particular effect or phenomena.

God's power is for evangelism not personal experience

We know that the Holy Spirit will work in our lives to bring healing, deliverance, holiness and wholeness. But we must never forget that, ultimately, the power of the Spirit is given to help us be Christ's witnesses.

John 16:8 shows that the Spirit comes to *'convict the world of sin, and of righteousness, and of judgment.'* Historically, revival phenomena have been experienced essentially in the context of evangelism and mission rather than in meetings for the saints. It is a great danger that churches which receive some blessing from God can so enjoy the experience that they forget the Spirit always wants us to focus on revealing Jesus to the world.

We should find that, as the Holy Spirit makes us more like Christ, we will want to share his life with others: this is a 'naturally supernatural' work of the Spirit.

Don't wait for God to give you more before you act on what you have received

Some people almost seem to be 'addicted' to a particular experience, and appear to be unable to do anything unless they first experience a particular phenomenon. Others request 'more power' or 'more anointing' when they have not used or moved out in the power that they have already received.

Whenever we receive from God in any way it is useful to ask ourselves why we have received it – and then to begin to use it for the purpose for which it was given.

We must remember that Jesus took a boy's few loaves and fish and multiplied them to feed thousands. Similarly, we must recognise that what we have already received can be used mightily by God.

Equally, we must not forget that the devil will always do anything – speak any lies – to persuade us not to carry out Christ's commission. He will often whisper to us that we won't be able to do this or that until we have had another dose of the latest experience.

But if we have been filled with the Spirit, we have all the resources of heaven at our disposal. We can move out in God's power and compassion, confident that

God will grant us all the gifts we need – when the needs arise.

Do everything to maintain the unity of the Spirit

I began this book with a plea that my words would not be used in a negative way against anyone who may differ from my conclusions. For I believe that we should always prize our unity most highly – it too precious and too important a gift to spoil.

Sadly, there are always those who value their opinions more than their relationships in Christ – and those who put their experience before their oneness. We must remember that, when God pours out his blessing, the devil will always seek to destroy that work – and disunity is his favourite weapon. We must do everything to maintain the unity of the Spirit.

The heart of the gospel is reconciliation, and unity is its essential expression. We are inconsistent when we profess that we are passionate about the work of the Spirit yet half-hearted about oneness.

If we are to keep in step with the Spirit we must openly acknowledge that unity is God's present purpose for the church – and then align our actions with our words. We must stop criticising those brothers and sisters with whom we disagree about non-essential matters. If Jesus prayed that we will be one so that the world will know the truth, our refusal to stand with a brother or sister actively holds up evangelism. Even the pagans unite with those they agree with.

We have seen that every true manifestation of the Spirit builds the church up by building it together. And we know that God's building grows as we are knit together in love.

Personally, I am sure that God has visited us in recent days with startling blessing. I am equally certain that there is much, much more to come in the future. However, we do need to see the fruit of the Spirit developing from our encounters with God. And love is at the heart of the fruit.

Those of us who genuinely experience a touch from God must aim to build up the whole body rather than our own small part. We will be characterised by love, not slander; by self-effacement, not ambition; by gracious tolerance, not theological bigotry; and by common appreciation, not critical arrogance.

Moreover, we will be filled with a constant sense of wonder at Christ's great sacrifice for us – and with a burning passion to share his gospel of grace with the lost around us.

It is my fervent prayer that Habakkuk 3:2–3 will be prayed again and answered again in our own days.

'O Lord, revive your work in the midst of the years! In the midst of the years make it known; in wrath remember mercy.

God came...'

'Oh for the fire to fall again – fire which shall affect the most stolid! Oh, that such fire might first sit upon the disciples, and then fall all around! O God, thou art ready to work with us today even as thou didst then. Stay not, we beseech thee, but work at once. Break down every barrier that hinders the incoming of thy might! Give us now both hearts of flame and tongues of fire to preach thy reconciling word, for Jesus' sake. Amen.'   (C.H. Spurgeon)

If you have enjoyed this book and would like to help us
to send a copy of it and many other titles to needy
pastors in the **Third World**, please write for further
information or send your gift to:

Sovereign World Trust
PO Box 777, Tonbridge
Kent TN11 9XT
United Kingdom

or to the **'Sovereign World'** distributor in your country.

If sending money from outside the United Kingdom,
please send an International Money Order or Foreign
Bank Draft in STERLING, drawn on a **UK** bank to
Sovereign World Trust.